T0158698

SNOWMELT

Snowmelt

SNOWMELT

Poems by Shaun T. Griffin

Illustrations by Karen Kreyeski

Rainshadow Editions, The Black Rock Press
University of Nevada, Reno   1994

Printed in the United States of America

Cover art and illustrations by Karen Kreyeski
Used with permission of the artist

Rainshadow Editions
The Black Rock Press
University Library/322
University of Nevada, Reno 89557-0044

The publication of this book was supported, in part,
by the, C.I.T.Y. 2000, Reno Arts Commission.

C.I.T.Y. 2000
RENO ARTS COMMISSION

For Debby and Nevada

Your voices enabled me
to slip nightly
into words

and

for Jess Yoshio Hayashi

old fisher-friend
you swim
here still

CONTENTS

In the Rough

Seized by Faces

Back Home

Foreword

Whether Shaun Griffin is familiar with Matthew Fox, the famous radical Roman Catholic theologian, I don't know. But certainly Fox would salute Griffin as a friend of Mother Earth and the follower of the Cosmic Christ. Griffin is a leading Nevadan poet, who, of course, loves his state. He would turn his painterly eye on whatever state happened to be his home. Whether it is the subtle sign of bitter winter on an August day, or the delicate contours of an autumn leaf, or the delightful promise of warmth beside his wife's warm legs, Griffin helps us share his sensation.

Even as he shares his homeland with us, Griffin takes us on his travels away from home. We experience how "The loneliest road in America" must be. He speaks with some scorn of "the prattle of a book on blue roads," a way of referring to it that is a bit painful to those who have the wasteful hope of finding companionship in solitude. But Griffin seeks and finds it with people.

He finds it with the outcast, the downtrodden, the oppressed. Yet in the poem "Social Work" he expresses his grief and frustration over it. He confesses "I would cry at days' end." He has done a great deal of work with the disabled and the arts. In his own way he makes the dumb speak and the lame dance. I once asked him whether he had a family member who was disabled. No, he said, it's just something he's always wanted to do. I dearly wish though, that he had written a poem about this important aspect of his life. Certainly, he does not consider the disabled as among the downtrodden. Glory be to his vision! Most people have no vision of the disabled at all.

But it is the last section of this book that Griffin the lover excels. His spare, muted love for his wife and two boys almost makes my idols Gerald Manley Hopkins and Dylan Thomas well-nigh gaudy. But poor Hopkins feared his love of men might sully his love for God, or more precisely, imperil God's love for him, and Thomas drowned love and life itself. Griffin sees God in love and life, and life and love in God, healthy and free of hang-ups.

Vassar Miller

Preface

Beginning with the first poem "Virginia City, 1983," this collection spans five years, and reflects many changes during that period. Most obvious, is the birth of a son, the years spent away at graduate school, and finally our return to northern Nevada. The three sections in the book are arranged in a thematic order to give the reader a sense of this journey, if that is the right word for growing older.

Someone once said all writing is personal, and these poems are no exception. However, it has grown increasingly difficult for me to record things out of context when so often they are woven into a much larger picture. That is to say, the politics of poverty have found their way into my art, or rather, I couldn't find any other way out of the lives with whom I work and the stories they share.

The voices, the people on these pages are part of a fabric from which I drew the original idea of *Snowmelt*. The title is from a great fishing trip with my departed friend Jess. Snow was melting everywhere, things began to thaw; a return to warmth after a deep winter. In many ways, the spring run-off was like the full cycle of change in this book, and thus the closing poem "If You Are Unable." Here's to the circles we travel in!

Shaun T. Griffin

Acknowledgments

The author gratefully acknowledges the following publications, in which some of these poems originally appeared: "Poetic Drive" in *The Meadows*, 1982; "In a Sparse Tone" in *The Meadows*, 1983, and *In Writing*, 1984; "Snowmelt" in *Pinchpenny*, 1986; "Married Student Housing" in *EdVents*, 1987; "Virginia City, 1983" and "A Taste of March on the Comstock" in *The Comstock Chronicle*, 1987, 1988; "In December Steam" in *Bristlecone*, 1988; "A Place of Stone" in *The Redneck Review of Literature*, 1988; "Beneath a Pacific Moon" in *Interim*, 1988; "Bolillo Man" in *Bristlecone*, 1990; "On Highway 50" and "On the San Francisco Zephyr" in *Seven Nevada Poets*, Rainshadow Editions, Black Rock Press, University of Nevada, Reno, 1991.

Major funding for the publication of this book was provided by the C.I.T.Y. 2000 Reno Arts Commission. Their generous support is gratefully acknowledged.

The author would like to thank Carolyn Kizer and Vassar Miller for their stubborn insistence on the most musically precise words to dance in a poem. To Richard Shelton and Hayden Carruth, a heroic cheer for their belief in young poets. He also extends heartfelt thanks to the following individuals: his parents, Daniel and Jean, for their unwavering support from the beginning; John Garmon whose encouragement with this book was critical; Sam Hamill, whose thoughtful words were deeply appreciated, though he did not know it; Bill Musgrave, for his many readings of these poems in Palo Alto coffeehouses; Maxine Cirac, dear neighbor and proofreader, and Bob Blesse, who made all of this possible.

Finally, thank you to Karen Kreyeski, an artist and seeress whose haunting images of the Comstock mountains brings a stunning depth of vision to *Snowmelt*.

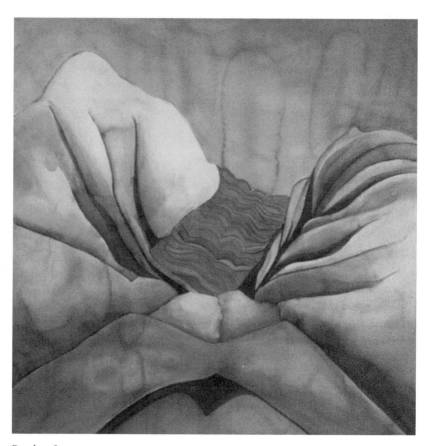

Road to Sutro

In the Rough

Virginia City, 1983

I say goodbye to the piñon—
sage of the Comstock,
trill of meadowlark at dawn

the red-orange rock
hardened in resin of years,
golden land, blown down

and clapboard house,
burnt with sun and snow,
sloped on a mountain.

Mine tailings drift
sculpt face of Chinese labor,
scrub memory to the grave.

Rich, purple arms of the Sierra
bristle with Jeffrey, sugar pine,
streams in homeward snowmelt.

The veil of herb on wind
perforates air with silver leaf,
rooted symbol of desert tension—

the tale told among leaves
will cease to unfold;
I must leave for still life of city.

Snowmelt

for Jess Hayashi

I came for an evening and a day
of fishing. I caught Jeffrey pines
arched in the Shasta sky
and the rage of water from the boat,
snowmelt, in the silver mouth
  of a stream.

Your eyes were so rich and brown
as you held the smallmouth bass in your hand
and pronounced, "All bones, nothing to eat,"
then flung her over the tip of your rod
to the chill green water below.
A splash and it was gone.

The flutter of a minnow
kept the four-pound test alive
till the snap of a rainbow
brought you over the bow.
The reel shed line
with each quiver of the hook
but you worked that trout to the end.

We cleaned the fish on the bulkhead
at Salt Creek. The pilings from the pier
rose like splinters in the water; they warmed
more darkness than I care to tell.

Begonia Lucerna

You came to this place
a wrinkled eight inch stick
in the bottom of a suitcase—
darkness for days of travel.
You were born in the thick
Welsh earth of Tenby
and now you are here,
just a shoot above
the chill Pacific waters
of the Peninsula.

I watch your skin
spiral into leaves
the color of rhubarb
and nurture the fetal tendrils
through their first
moist weeks of transition.

Still, how still
the departure from roots:
a leaf wakes with red light.
Wet wings in the air,
they perform a fragrant etching
on lines so thin
and circles faintly silvered
as if the damp walls
of this clay pot
were turned toward Tenby.

All the Worthwhile Things

are in bed, swirling
above my good friend's head
in a vase of roses
she nightly gives to me
with the awkward satisfaction
of a flower girl at a wedding.

Always, I play down her dreams
knowing the wind nearly howled
me to death last night; she only
stirred, slipped somewhere
beneath the covers
as a sand dollar
might slip beneath the sea.

I awoke to find the porch
curiously strewn with leaves
and paper— all the clutter
of a high desert storm. She drank
coffee on the steps
knowing also, I would sweep them
then sit beside her warm brown legs
for want of a fire.

We shoveled little pools
in the earth where our toes
could rest, and waited for
the sun to awaken speech.
At last, I realized there was none:
she was alone and dreaming
peacefully about the roses.
And I? I was beside her
dreaming of us.

sycamore

gray fingers
reach out

mark the ground
with shadow

empty of leaf
light or lesson

a supple arch
to the earth

so damp
in winter

On Highway 50

The loneliest road
in America—

Life Magazine

She lies on a plain of sagebrush
and chipped blue asphalt
making its way
to the nowhere edge of Nevada.
I drive this road and she

crawls to the periphery
of my vision
as if she were looking
for someone to speak with.
I feel empty

at the turnout on Highway 50.
The railroad sign
stirs in the wind
and some unknown offspring
of the desert says, "No,

don't leave me.
I have waited with the sand
in my mouth for years
and still I am no more
than a thread of desire."

A Place of Stone

for Ben and Karen

I come for the wooded dance of the Comstock:
the piñon pine, harsh as the face of an owl,
juniper, a scruff beard on the high desert,
and locust, spent, with purr of cicadas.

I come alone, in a blue-black forest of night,
steal my way into the folds of darkness,
risk ruin under the light of a star. I come
as so many others must, for that which is missing
from the stencil of the city: the outline of a face
on the back of a horse, the quiet rocks
that grow and grow in the sun's burnt strokes,
and the pine nuts glazed with sap in fall.

I come for the fissures that ripple through this land:
the empty spell of a mine shaft, water
dripping in like a slow clock from above;
the breaking, the chipping, the bloody salt smells
that ride the canyons. A trail of ashen dreams
flake the golden skin of Nevada.

I come to fill the fallow contours of my mind
with a place of stone, yet nearly everything
has been stripped from these slopes.
Even the cornflowers cower in the tailings.
Cattle graze on winter roots and a farmer
fingers heat from the stove.
Fences crawl over half-bleached plains,
touch the moon's corrosive light

and I return, a wisp of desert wood.

Poetic Drive

Somewhere north of Lone Pine on 395,
almost as far from home as I can stand
and still be happy, back slouched
in a blue pickup, I steer

into a soft, red light, as if to undress
in the car's silhouette
and play with the only thing I know.
And what, but a stack of words—

a postcard's worth, for the journey home.
I push them into dreaded line,
eke sense out of tiny bodies. They flail
on a hot wind. Somehow not distracted

by distant beams or motor's moan,
they poem for me, once again.

Decomposition

It's cold and gray and winter
outside. The leaves starve
as they fall to the ground.
Snow rustles as they move
to darkness, and for once
the earth is white, just white
enough to crowd a browned

and broken leaf into obscurity.
The soil pickles its young,
desiccates birds of prey.
A January wind
pierces limbs like a pitchfork,
shakes the last dead leaves from stems,
and eats them till they become snow,

or rain, sliced in spring.

Beneath a Pacific Moon

I am leaving for the other side.
Faces wait for me to cross
a line we have drawn over land.

I have told them of this place
beneath a Pacific moon
but they cannot understand me.

The ocotillo has died
over streets of sand
and dark hands reach
for their spines
like shadows on the desert floor.

The hot wind is a shaman
from the mountains of Sonora.
Each day it comes
for the red rock of San Felipe
and this is the way I choose:

toward the border, toward the faces
that wait for me there.

Bajo una luna pacífico

Voy a partir al otro lado.
Caras esperan para cruzar
una línea hemos dibujado sobre tierra.

Ya les he contado de este lugar
bajo una luna Pacífico
pero ellos no pueden entenderme.

El ocotillo ha muerto
sobre calles de arena
y manos morenas tratan de cojer
sus espinas como sombras
en el suelo del desierto.

El viento caliente es un brujo
de las montañas de Sonora.
Cada día viene
por la piedra roja de San Felipe
y éste es el camino que elejí:

hacia la frontera, hacia las caras
que me esperan allá.

on a january morning

sun
you linger through
the faded strands of sycamore
on a january morning

you survive
the felted ice that clings
to every shingle above my head

you light the rising
and falling of my ways
a shadow from the narrow
leafless vines of ivy

sounds at sunrise
a cackle like a magpie raving
over a rabbit in the road

you will say no for grief's sake

the light will enter
without the raving bird
or the vine's frail visit to the ground

your ephemera
will wander into this place
like equatorial light at dawn

and the spider's web
carefully dusted with dew
will spread again
reticulate

A Taste of March on the Comstock

On days like this,
the sun burns snow
from a damp and weary earth,
sets fire to the last traces of winter,
and the bulbs break
into an early morning stretch.

A windchime flies
in the chill mountain air,
and the weighted back
of a lone Scotch pine
cracks the frozen drifts.
Beneath layers of sod,

the first sprigs of rye
pop from roots, separate
and send, a melting family
of snow and ice
back to the dark confines
of a waiting, winter cloud.

Morning Ritual

The paper plays upon my thoughts.
Columns swell with an early sun.
Stories rise from the page
in a warm spiral of light—
candles I cannot burn.
Fresh faces toil with shadows
from a spring sky.
I release them
to the natural rage of clouds,

squirrel along headlines,
then retreat to smolder
of good weather.
Words fly over my fingers,
float to the floor.
Nothing in this room
but space, still space for
words. I am confused to state:
they are small to touch.

Unable to elude empty squares,
I turn heat from the ink,
listen for screams in the margin.
Black details of classified, obituary
kindle and crack fire
in wood stove.
Soot pours over brown grass.
The paperboy will ride early
with his canvas bag.

I spread coffee on the table
and lie in wait: print pales at dawn.

Fence Post

Under dark swallows of sun
a wordsmith hammers,
rails a 16 penny
to a redwood post.
The tremor of wood fades.

He measures out six feet
spades the earth
with salmon thumbs,
the trail of honey light
wedged between his fingers.

Limbs, barren from the travel
of years, he severs
sage root with an axe,
drapes a plumb line
from a cloudless sky
and staggers the fall of cement.

The level slides from palm
to post. He pricks
the corners with pencil:
red beams on a sanded floor,
then sights the last hole.
He drags dust on a desert wind.

The shovel stings as it drops:
the clang of rock drives him
to his hands. He slides the pick
under stone, the earth splinters,
and eight feet of redwood
rise in a straight line of fence.

The Winded Order of this Place

It's the supple wood I crave:
the squirrel's powdered cache,
needles in granite crags over water,
a windless ripple on fog-bound lake.

Beneath a forest of dusted light
the raven cover of silence,
night more black than skin, and air,
a frail rain listing at my face.

I trail the spine of Jeffrey
to its knotted end; atop a feathered branch
the wild ring of a mountain jay, a mad cackle
in the winded order of this place.

Fall's first full bloom: the German brown
have receded to the depths; orange blossom
of aspen and birch trench the earth
with color; frost chafes at the roots.

A wet limb spins itself to the ground,
I spin with it, sway in the motionless gray
of morning, collect dry spell of sleep;
lie flat with supple woods all around.

On the San Francisco Zephyr

A diesel dons its black plume,
fences grate at the dust.
This train rides through backyards.
Scrap metal and glass
twist along the tracks;
boxcars bent on siding grass.

The passengers read
like a menu: hot, bland, or broken.
I return to the prattle
of a book on blue roads. Sun
dangles fingers in my scalp,
deadens the insistent clatter

of steel. Faces turn to wheels,
roll me back
to the icy edge of Nevada.
For so little, I would travel
your desolate arteries
to the end, but oh, America

the rails slap beneath me
and I cannot find a pulse.

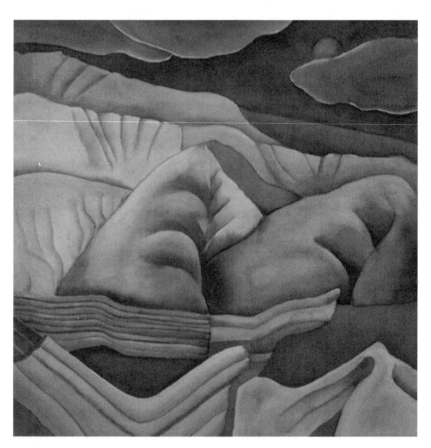

Walk with the Cougar

Seized by Faces

Oh Gentle Poem

wary of the way the world works,
I come back to you
for the musical words,
words that sting the eye,
and nuance of shape
that lets you slip
in and out of things concrete.

Oh gentle poem
color of flesh and marrow.
Let light in, if you will,
let light in
the small frames of existence;
work the thin line through my bones,
break all that fills with despair.

Oh gentle and turning poem
dance among the ink
of weary eyes.
Surround me with rhythm!
Strike the living
into sounds
that I can bear.

Mother

for J. C.

She strays from her room
to socialize. The children move
as if an oil lamp
burns in her eyes. They look
for a sign on her thin lips.
She fills a glass to breathe in Byron
on the sloped chair. At her back
braids fall in their hands.

After the glow of vermouth
they reach for her palms.
Languid sea stories
slide from her mouth.
They do not hear her.
She returns
with his blue hat and gloves.
Seven years ago, he left
for the iron skin of a freighter.

She quietly works
the sweet cadence of "Darkness"
from the page:
"This is what I gave him."
Nothing so full as flesh
to shroud her from their eyes.
Even the trance of liquid
fails. She fights the gray light
of stars. Tiny faces circle her bed,

linger in the Romantic rhythm
of her dreams.

In a Sparse Tone

for Richard Shelton

In the quiet areas
where speech will never come
I hear your footsteps
reaching out on the dry
Sonoran wind, making those
desperate desert sounds
that one must make
to survive where the sun
and the sand meet
like two parched lips
on the horizon.

I wonder then, if
it isn't you, dear Richard
who is weeping
over the warm apricot earth
quietly filling your
freckled hands with tiny
pools of melancholy
or concern, or just plain fear
that nothing will ever
grow to enchant you
like the playful path

of a desert creek gone dry.

Conference

The sound you made was a
hoarse and fitful bleating.

Stanley Kunitz

I wonder what it felt like,
heat from a November sky.
Inside the dry walls of this hotel
since dawn; no sun from the podium.
Nameless faces feed me coffee,
note places beyond the glass.
I peer through portals in their house.

Last night, the spare voice
of a poet: "luminous, natural and deep."
He sculpted the death of a whale
on a winter beach, dangled snakes
from a tree above his garden,
dredged a bay for its final remorse.
He moved among us like driftwood.

Today, I ponder the material light
of a salesman. Nothing moves
but a face of gray eyes,
red hair. He swings the tail
of a spotted tie, points at charts, trade secrets.
If only he warmed his pale drawl,
shed color on the black vines of speech.

If only he heard the whale's cry.

The Incision of Distance

for K. B.

The road has cut between us
with white-line precision:
you there, me here—
no way to huddle or converse
and play what we found
so good in each other,
an easy refrain of laughter.

Wedged in a bright, orange booth,
we jangled dreams over sausage and hotcakes;
the window was fogged with breath.
Now, I reach you through a piece of plastic.
Wind wails in the microphone,
your voice trickles in.
We straddle the minutes alone.

A scant three hours by car,
it may as well be Maine, or Missouri.
I know you had to leave;
the weather and all. Something torn
or disfigured on the horizon,
we met by chance and cracked fire
in this cold, cold place.

Reptilian, we shed dry skin
and slithered home to family. Were you
any closer, it would do them no good.
You came to this place a friend.
I wade in the slumber of memory,
set foot on a broken highway
where chilled, we once stood.

Memory of a Son

She tremors in denim and flat shoes.
His bone-white face looms
at the door. The seconds turn
like cloves between her fingers.

The key turns light on her beige skin.
She sails portholes of the past:
a college bride, steadied with firm
olive eyes; words of love trail off.

His red eyes churn silence
from the glass; her hand
cold as the cubes. He reels in a storm
of news black and white.

They chant a tattered grace;
he bears down on lamb, she prefers
greens before meat. A knife crosses
the plate where their son sat.

The sheets are tucked and crisp
where his fingers once ran.
At bedside, they gather speech
for a broken womb—

a heroic catholic whisper,
and haul sleep from a petulant moon.

Bolillo Man

for A. C.

Four a.m., a scratch of sun, fire
in a brick oven, wood heat
for hours after ash. The flour sack
turns from the wall, sugar and salt,
water to sleeve the white mass. He palms
the short red cloth at his waist,
cups supple mounds on a long, bleached paddle—
each loaf, slit with a razor to bloom once baked. Feet
flush to cement, he flutters from scaffle
to scaffle of dough, looses them on the earthen floor.
Rows of wheat mushroom, crust and slope
like clay. He towels his forehead, bends,
and rakes crumbs from the powder bowl.

His wife culls from soft,
brown shapes, scrapes to basket
the eldest son's portion. "They're not heavy
when they're hot," and fits the cotton pad
to his head. He reels beneath the creaking reeds,
softens, and teeters away.
A guanábana drops to the porch,
rolls to certain death. The Doña peels pesos
from her bra; the second son has returned.
Tourists fill the town; the bolillo man
knows how they eat. She is skeptical,
sends out her third boy for a final trip.

At wave's edge, they prick loaves;
barter for bread to be taken.
The coins slide into a plastic bag;
vibrate to a dull clang— nothing can strip

the sound from his ears
save father's countenance.
In ten warm hours, thirty kilos of flour
have risen to a faint hunger.
He closes the newspaper
over the oven's tiny mouth, wipes eyes dry
draws water from the appliance.
The midday heat scowls;
sweet smoke, still at last.

Thien Hong*

for V. N.

The sun rises in black circles
above a silver roof and plywood walls.
He touches the skin of each child
as if a flower, waits for breath
to stir dreams from their heads.

The kitchen fills with steam,
green tea kindles their spry limbs.
She kneads the flesh of the youngest,
his bones, a frail tribute
to the camp he was born in.

He peels the sheet from window frame,
the clatter of children muffle
a barbed vision of water's edge.
It tears through light as if
a seam to the world outside.

The car bursts forth with a blue cloud.
Faces huddle in back. Wiper blades strip dew
from glass. She brings it to a stop;
his eyes are dark as coal. He shouts
"Goodbye!" The others crawl out at schools

drawn gray and damp from age. In class
she studies the crooked rules of syntax;
her voice, flush with desire
from a stolen land. At work,
her husband crowds a file room desk,

*red sky

29

pages the still life of numbers
in pink and yellow stacks.
When his boss yells, he recoils:
the mouths rise up from the ashen floor
of memory, anger clots his throat.

"You could feed them for six weeks—"
a co-worker's admonition spins
at the base of his neck. Rings
coil about him, throb lower back
where caged, they kicked for seven years.

Her words come softly to him:
"Without you, we have no one."
On break, he sips coffee with cream,
presses the limits of language:
"I learn Latin as a boy, speak French,

teach math—, route purchase orders—"
At preschool, she catches the small face.
He splashes sand on the tires,
climbs to her arms. They journey home,
ginger teems with chicken. The two bedrooms

are quiet; the boy sleeps, she reads
from a notebook. The lines blur
with phrases. Her tongue turns upward,
splits sound as it crests the palate,
blooms, and slides to the floor.

Her eldest daughter feeds the washer
as it bobs in dark clay.
The machine dances against sheetrock.
Tomatoes, peppers and parsley
crowd the damp borders of trees.

Sun filters in the basement,
invoices come to a clean, sorted stop.
Manila folders climb shelves to the ceiling.
He gathers lunch sack, overshirt,
and plies the pavement to a familiar link fence.

Shouts pour from the house.
At the door, he holds her thin arms,
turns, settles to a chill beer.
A game show rankles from a swollen night stand,
the boys fight like jackals at his feet.

The youngest crawls to this chest,
lifts the bulky glasses overhead.
She scuttles a towel at the waist,
they sit below a cross on the mantle.
The sheet comes down the window.

Fog spills in from the bay.
A faint cry from the back room,
he whispers to a small face, tracks the wood
to bed. She sleeps without notice;
he finds breath at his side.

The Dancing Tree

Sweet residue of failure
hangs from a floral stage.
The hardwood floor is streaked
with sweat. Aisles fill with faces.

He is a moon at their backs
unable to choreograph its rising.

Already the makeup is beading:
skin slit with color to create
a bark; lines drawn over nose, mouth
and eye, deciduous shapes run wild.

Warm cloth stretches down his spine,
supple foliage behind green slippers—
one touch and they fall, leaves
from a dancing tree. Great limbs

carry his shudder to the seated,
who have come to break

from the ground. They step away,
an awkward trellis of motion, as if
to gray the final scene. He is wet now,
water on the seam of a bough.

Woman Empty

On her heart
a growth flames
with hatred.
In a room, numb with men
she is too weak
for the stench of passion.

They want more
than tented thighs
and pearl skin. Hard hands
rake a bed of coals;
breathe the blood
of her legs.

The seed spins like rice
at her waist.
She screams for the face
of a friend;
they rack flesh
with fingers of stone.

In December Steam

in memory of John Lennon

December 8, 1986

Six years ago today, beneath the iron gate of the Dakota
you fell from the world. Made lead
by the hands of a psychotic fan, gun more surreal
than candles on the sewer grate. All night,
the irrational chorus of voices, chanting
"All we are saying—"

New York, an anonymity on the Upper West Side:
the clouds of protest, gone from the street.
A song drifts like a humid wind and you
are riding the crest of a lyric more painful
than the tears we broke for you. We reel
from the rhythm, our psyche, blind at the altar.

Sacrifice, the window through which you spoke,
your playful stroll in December steam
transfixed on a vision of peace. Imagine war
gone like ice from our lives! hunger and greed,
a levee spilled over. Singing the dream
of one flesh, you walked in this world.

A raven boy called out, "Father."
Fallen bird, you touched his wings.
The woman, so dark in her repose, kindled heart
in your eyes. Flush with family, the sound
was hopeful. At forty, a fantasy
for the radio waves. And we nearly let go—

but nothing prepared us for your passing
save the riddled speech of a bent, subway rider.

Separation

Her legs burn in a plume of dust.
She cannot understand the climbers.
On a switchback to the ridge-line
they mark the ponderosa with cloth.

Beneath a single lodgepole pine
she waits for water from the creek.
Nothing comes. Only the first rustle
of sage. Names float on the lake

tell her when the moon will crest
the bay. Black figures move
on the trailhead, lift shadows
from trees and cut circles in the air

with breath. Fixed on a point below
she is a cairn at water's edge.
A cone splits the earth with seed.
Shards of granite tear from the bowl

and she follows their stiff, dry fall
to earth, flails her feet to rest.

While Stones Rage

At the Vietnam Veterans Memorial,
Washington, D.C.

Pencils arc names of the deceased,
release them from the terror of black stone.
In the lexicon of war, letters dance:
no sound in the lives that perch
among the newsprint, the aging metal stars.

Vietnam! a verb that will not die;
silk work in the minds of a generation:
remorse lies furrowed in marble lines
that flower among street vendors,
and limestone walls beyond.

Fervent the settling rock, patched into earth,
treated, retreated like nausea from afar.
Nothing disturbs the quiet language of fear;
it reels on, the horror of young men,
minds gone to the garden of red light.

On the horizon, a bloated rucksack
in rain forest of verb *to be.* Fresh names
soothe the spring of honor;
stones rage in the memory
of short lives, guns muted in wonder.

Under the Tented City of Hebron

"...it means you're fighting children."

Lt. Col. Moshe Givati
Israeli commander on the West Bank

You live under a military tent
your street a bramble of wire and steel.
Grazed in the face with a camera
you recede in a picture flown to the free.
A four-year-old on the front page

with no one to visit her caged city.
I read of death's voice in the paper:
"What am I doing here? Is it right?"
the commander squeals to a reporter.
We are left to ingest the dilemma of Hebron.

We eat from the floor of your eyes;
you are not there, only bone and fear
rise from the portrait. What will it be
this time— death on a movie screen
to shed the green skin of soldiers?

You cannot speak through the clang of rifles
and blur in a careful, knotted hunger
unable to return the steel gesture of arms.
We drift among hands in the rubble
lost but for the flesh on the barrel.

You transcend our failure to hide
like white wine at the table of twelve—
a good God that cannot relinquish us from pain.
We know of its killing ways, have watched stones fall
for centuries. Now you crumble in the dust.

Saturday Night in Palo Alto

standing room only in Printer's Inc.,
a sanctuary for the common, literary cold.
Wedged in the pine shelves of Thoreau and Marx,
the patrons reflect in long breaths
so as not to flutter their pastoral eyes.

Mozart churns like smoke among the stacks.
A lanky, trench-coat fellow remarks,
"Wolfgang lived in a *great* era—"
At the discount table, a glimmer
among the sweet, educated smiles.

In most college towns, Saturday night
is a time for the smooth skin of one's love.
In Palo Alto, that's almost a book,
or the ritual of *looking at books*
in the quiet of Printer's Inc.

The Contours of Travel

Mosquito, fat with my blood—
you pierce flesh
with a thin, brown needle,
thrash ankles with vile antigen.
Each day, a new red clot
festers beneath damp skin.
I measure your fired presence
with wings at my feet.

Equatorial land:
green, glowing green!
rain, spilt to a heated floor.
The bites swell to a warm blue.
Fluid cracks from a pore;
flecks of sand
tease its beaded flow,
white cells stream in.

I page a pale book
through light unfiltered.
You etch and infect as I rest
to a great scroll of sky.
A cartographer of pulse and marrow—
you must fly, dear lady
to be weighted by blood—
come script the arch and heel.

Face of Light

for E. L.

She sleeps alone for comfort;
no one can hold her— not I
nor the doctors, nor the shrewd minds
of science. Not one to calm the muscles
that rattle flesh to dawn.

Her shrill cry lashes out
like a woman in labor.
And what to make of the stars?
such bright signs on a canvas
colored with moonlight—

The ritual of longing for daybreak
is over; she rests in shaded light.
Moments drift to morning,
flush adrenalin through her veins
and soon, the hands return

for pulse, fluid or pressure,
and inevitably, turn away
to meter progress on a chart.
She pulls at the curtains
that shroud her existence

day after receding day; colors the room
with sun. If not for her vision
of a tranquil flesh, not one
could rise to still
the faint marks of its passing.

The Counsel of the Rain

I listen to the offbeat counsel
of the rain. It falls through
the cracks of shelter, slips
down unknown faces,
into the icy pool of existence.

A cold percussion
distills thoughts from gray light.
In a damp forest of the living
the psyche's blue seams
rock the water for food.

Social Work

I cannot shake their faces.
They clammer through a sleepless night.
For so long, the shards of voices—
even as I draw closer to the edge.

Their lives are blistered
with children, bad checks
and pain-killing hatred
for the one that got them there.

And I, a feeling-stone
for those who must lay
down their emotions
in the sterile comfort of an office.

They form lines
long before I arrive,
chart the path that separates
from job, home or spouse.

If, it ended there, if
I could thwart their anger
with the crude tools of this profession,
if I could turn from the vile

fragments of their speech,
if, I could return the frail volley—
if, it ended there
I would cry at day's end.

A Metered Vision

We asked to be obsessed
with writing, and we were.

Robert Lowell

You fell from the back seat
of a New York cab
with eyes so intense
that nothing, save death, could enter.
Was it the lens of the lithium,
or were you speaking to us
that day we learned
the shrill comfort of your silence?

References to Thoreau and thorazine
were scattered like dice
among the women,
the poets, and the family
who almost endured
your sleepless nights to the end.

In your arms, a lone
metered vision gathers still.

Son of a Broken Man

for P.

Oh compadre, I long to tear
the mourning from your voice,
rid you of father's terror;
though I cannot, I wish it—
your sealed hands swerve for touch.

In the spring, when snow cracks
you will pore over its melting face,
clutch ice as if tears: fallen
stricken with sun, touch ice
and rejoice in a clear, cold shadow.

And your lungs, though wintered
will whisper poetry from the black vines
of El Paso, city of dust, death and origin.
You will speak to the mandrake of his eyes,
wrest grief from the pupil, travel to heart's end.

You will lift words to a broken palate,
scrape moisture from red lips
pinch fingers between vertebrae—
the pair of you, released
will set fear adrift in warm, salt tears.

Homecoming

Back Home

portrait of a lady

for deborah

soft
would have been
the sound i heard

slight
the color
i saw seep in the room

wan
the eyes
that watched me move

sweet
the lips
pressed on my tongue

smooth
the arms
pulled to my chest

still
the thoughts
that crept across your face

slow
the smile
that swayed before me

sunlight
between us
on that first fragile morning

the womb purple

1

your eyes
    still
as the water
   in a cool
stream-fed pond

    breath
    fragile
as a bird

fingers
 trail
 like tendrils
in the sun

      sleep
has overcome you

  a soft
shoot of air
  whirls
in your veins

   you rest
in a warm
   San Antonio
       breeze
  lie so peacefully
  it seems
you have left us

returned
 to a womb
more still
  than the gaze

     so delicate
  upon your life

2

your mother
   would have colored
     the womb purple

   it was all
     she could do

 to let you kick
    at the seams
of her skin
   for nine months

    now
      we watch
   rapt
as the blue lines
            pulse
    in your face

marvel
  at the sleepy ways
     you flush
        to the whir
           of pepper corns

as we slip
        ever deeper
    into your
grasp

Yen

I face silence
the no-noise of lips
closed to the fingers of air
voice, or others who might enter.
Marvel at structure
on shoulders, cheeks,
quivers of bone, flesh—

Marvel at tremor on lips:
whisper of sound
full and resonant,
the pulse you make for living
dances down spine, through hands.
I feel vibration, a soft tongue
inches over face

rests in every corner of my mouth.
And forget how naked
we really are;
plunder out of silence
in a fetal grasp,
lie motionless
on the white skin of your navel.

The Last Beer in San Antonio

for W. and J.

*...the stream of creation and
dissolution never stops.*

Heraclitis

This could well be the last beer
I have in San Antonio:
a cool, refreshing Tecate
with limón y sal
perusing Joseph Campbell's
introduction to *The Portable Jung*
(how is it he lived in so many worlds?)
listening as my son rocks
himself to sleep
with the gentle purr
of the cooler in the background.

Where is it, San Antonio
that you have taken me?
Is it to your river's edge
so flush with life,
your migrant skies
fairly teeming with clouds,
or is it merely— away
from the stupor of a hardened land
I will never know?

Where is it, now that we
have worn our way
into your humid hands,
where is it, my dear San Antonio
now that the wild flowers have come down
for your houses,

where is it, with the plane ride so near
and the sheets you make for rain
waiting overhead?

Have you taken me too far, San Antonio,
too far from here? Must I return
so empty of your live oak forests,
mesquite fires, y fajitas al carbón?
Must I go home like this
now that you've slipped
so quietly through my senses?

I touch your words again, Dr. Jung
knowing we cannot return
to the makeshift room of ideas.
But they are not transient.
Rather, it is I who must leave
with so little to carry
save the heavy air.
of this sweet, Texas town.

Baja California Sur

for D. and S.

1

I finish a full moon
on the Sea of Cortés.
Waves break
as though wet lips,
brush silence
between people. At dawn
we tear clams from the reef
in a village no larger
than us.

You and I
have traveled to the end
of this peninsula
in search of a warm
Spanish sun, and now we are
with the saguaro, succulent
of the Sierra Madre,
and the lava flows
that drift so darkly to water.

The most we can hope for is wind;
at the very least
salted air
from the round stretch of sea.
What moisture to be had
is driven through sand
and even that, my friend
is spoken for. At land's edge
we are pitched in the ruin of stones.

2

We have brought our love
to be nourished
by the earthen roads and
clapboard cantinas,
to move among the cattle and lone
switch of snake;

have come to heal
our feeling for each other
even as the waves
crack still more shells
on the rocks below.

We come unfinished
as only one can,
to pretend
for these few days
that love is a soft orange sky
and you and I
its clouded followers.

We come to forget
our lives
have been kept like linens
in a smooth brown chest
and that before long
the labor of living alone
will set in
and our skin will go
from blue to gray.

3

There is no need to hide
from flesh.
It is only
the unnatural stillness
of life without you
I fear.

If, we should retrace steps
let it be you and I
who touch skin
to the waves.
If, we should hear their crack,
let it be on petals of sand
spun in the dry salt wind
that we fall.

And if, after the cold
quiver of years,
we should return
to this jagged place
let it be for a white string moon
or a clean summer rain.
Let the saguaro streak the earth
with green limbs,
and let us break down
and be broken into.

Farmhouse

You sleep on dream-curls of golden hair
coiled in a cold, slip-stream of voices.
Fingers travel meager rows of skin
streak the flesh with residue of first light.
Nothing is breached by the empty fields at your bedside.

You trespass the liniment of your mother's love,
trace black and white stills on the bureau,
her hand, wed to an American flyer after the war.
Sculpted in poverty, she quilts
in the earthen corner of the farmhouse.

Winter is stored in pockets of ice beneath the sill.
You scrape moisture from the surface as if to bevel
the glass. You woke to the silver dawn;
your hair, a strand of sepia on the furrowed horizon.

The World Is Small

when death comes:
we have only
their touch
to remember
what it was like.

The Cinnamon Cup

Flown from the back of a garden shed,
he sails the drive
with no wheel beneath his barrow.
It's chicken white and William's red—
a magic engine and he, its chief
dashing to fire.

He swings wide at the fence
tilts, and reels for the door,
sprung like an arrow
in small quivers of flight
a boy and his barrow
inches above the earth and tar.

How they fly
I am not to know.

There Is a Hurting Bone

You rake the hand with hurt,
slip bone from my grasp.

A brittle ache settles
in the mouth almost open.

Gray light floats from your eyes
like clouds after rain.

A cross-wind flutters
your voice to the floor

hollows the feet
you work down this path:

the uneven movement
of a life entwined.

The years are cracked
and swollen with feeling

marks of a past we choose
to keep breath in the room.

We turn flesh for the close-
ness of flesh, witness

the quiet travel of fingers
up the stem of a glass.

Through a bare, white palm
you utter this word love

follow stone-dark lines,
retrace skin we took.

It is a chilled path
we wander to redeem,

a habitual trail of feeling
gone awry, and back again

to the faint wind in your
soft, rippled mouth.

Father's Coral Heart

1

Raven boy holds her picture
at his fingertips.
Ash drops
on the border soil
of National City.
He grazes the hood,
jump-starts a '39 Ford
throttles the road to Mexico,
snaps every rule
like a sailor on leave.
Lights, dim as the moon
at dawn; her face
deep in the folds
of leather.

2

On his break
fingers dance on formica top.
A slide rule
splits the tension
of chemistry and rent,
bowling pins
hung by hand. Mother
teaches school; books
are loose in the kitchen.
A child turns
the Irish light in his eyes.

3

In windless heat
of garage, sweat
layered beneath his glasses,
chisel steadied
between thumb and forefinger,
he stoops over wood lathe,
crawls down the spine
of a dowel. The mahogany
spits curls of sawdust
up his forearms.
He smiles:
the plug firmly planted—
a desk, knotted for life.

4

Headstrong
at a steel desk,
fingers pinched like wire
on a circuit board,
he descends
into language of resistors.
Nothing to capture
the gentle twitch
of equations
save fresh green lines
on sketch paper.
A slim, white face
recedes, the veil
of corporate science.

5

A father
mired in middle age,
lashed to the family
by what he was.
He fingers the stairs
in beveled darkness.
Children linger
in front room portrait,
as if vines from the hearth.
He pieces, ever pieces
chambers together,
the ritual
of speechless ways.
His heart,
a great humidor
for kith and kin.

6

A sailor
stretched over the bilge
diesel in the grease
beneath his nails,
eyes brighter
than a jetty light in fog.
His face, warmed to a red
sky; nothing
to peel the moon away.
On the fly bridge,
he crests five foot waves,
cackles for the gulls. She
sands teak on her water house;
lives tarnish with sun.

7

Grandfather glistens
with his plump, blond boy.
The wagon jerks
with ten, fat fingers,
bumps down unpaved street.
Mother scatters dust from the porch.
He presses the moist skin
to his cheek,
whisper of new breath.

The life shed
that morning she moved:
hood, leather and ash,
faintly dress
his amber face.

To My Son

I will never feel you at my breast
as your mother feels you now.
Perhaps I will learn
the hungry ways of your mouth,
but for this moment, I must listen
to your whisper in her arms.

You have crept
into the warm speech of my sleep
and like so many fathers before me,
I make way for the tears
you speak to me
in the pearled darkness of the evening.

And when the movements in your flesh
begin to wake you,
we watch the first cracks of light
as they spill over our hair and skin,
and you, the writhing one,
reach to catch them
as they move across my face.

You catch my lips instead
and I tell you, that even now
at just six weeks
I cannot bear your absence.
I have come to rely
on the wind from your lips
as though it were flesh touching mine.
You shake me and I am reminded;
this is who you are:
this is how you move away from the womb

and follow the lines across our faces
to a life of your own, my son.

Married Student Housing

At dusk, the scratch of squirrel's feet.
Later still, the erratic shift of keys
linger in this cinderblock flat.
The two of us, bare in this place,
mark days with letters from friends.
We share voices, soiled with reason,
tire among the endless sounds
and lay our son upon us
in the plum light before dawn.

You and I travel these sterile rooms
like brother and sister.
The table is where you write;
I eat there and edit your lines.
We came here for an education.
We have received life without life
in the delicate hands of the learned.
Few expect us to return
short of breath and purpose.

Perhaps they are right. We have left
ourselves in three short years
and we will leave even more
at its conclusion. These things tread on;
another family will displace us
with their desire to learn.
And then we are reminded: we sleep
with the supple pounding of squirrels.
The walls are pale flesh now;

soon they will be brittle and faint,
a memory, skillfully dying among us.

Watch Him Walk

Walking out this morning with your
blond hair buried in a down vest
and the sky so gray we could touch it,
it was hard letting you go
harder still, watching
you tremble your way across
those broken orange leaves,
threading that thin line of balance
like you were being pulled away from me.

How is it you make your steps
so soft and unsure, wavering
all the while with those feet
barely large enough to hold you,
arms spinning like leaves from a tree
and your smile thicker than bluegrass?
You fairly made me cry
slicing the air with your life
so small. Oh my son, where
did you learn to walk like that?

Lying Awake without Us

I wonder who, among us
bites through dreams
of love torn down
in a heated cry.

(If only I could reach
her pale, moonlit shape.)

Or holds a face of sterile eyes
to a room, black with lines
from the dread.

(We breathe
harsh tones to the floor.)

Or who, without touch
to lead them, loosens
the stiff reins of skin.

(The clock snaps
to a halting rhythm.)

The stars drench words with feeling;
they settle like dust in the sill.
I wonder who, among us
wakes to their fallen presence.

If You Are Unable

to gather
any further
hue and cry
look not within
but remark
that it has passed
and journey
simply, home.

The Author

A Southern Californian by birth, Shaun T. Griffin ran a drop-in center for Hispanic youth while working toward his B.A. in psychology and M.S. in counseling at California State University, Fullerton. He taught psychology and creative writing at Western Nevada Community College from 1978 to 1983, and currently directs Nevada's homeless youth education office. In addition, he teaches a poetry workshop at Northern Nevada Correctional Center and has participated in many programs to bring poetry into the state's schools. His first collection of poems, *Words I Lost at Birth*, was published in 1981. He has travelled widely throughout Mexico and collaborated on a number of English/Spanish translations of poetry and fiction. In 1992 he received, with Emma Sepúlveda, the Carolyn Kizer Foreign Language and Translation Prize from *Calapooya Collage*. He is also the editor of two collections of poetry which have been published by the University of Nevada Press: *Torn by Light, Selected Poems of Joanne de Longchamps* (1993) and *Desert Wood, An Anthology of Nevada Poets* (1991). Shaun Griffin is considered by most to be one of Nevada's finest poets—he is, without question, the greatest advocate of the state's poetic heritage. He lives in Virginia City with his wife Debby and his two boys, Nevada and Cody, where they can see beyond the Dead Camel Mountains, one of the finer place names in northern Nevada.

Colophon

Designed by Robert E. Blesse at the Black Rock Press, University of Nevada, Reno Library, using Aldus PageMaker. Assistance provided by John Balkwill. The text typeface is Minion, designed by Robert Slimbach, with titling in Berthold Wolpe's Albertus. The text paper is acid-free. Film output by Reno Typographers. Printed and bound by BookCrafters, Chelsea, Michigan.